TOURNAMENT FIGHTING

The Techniques, Training Drills
and
Strategy of Open Competition

By Keith Vitali

©UNIQUE PUBLICATIONS INC., 1984
All rights reserved
Printed in the United States of America
ISBN: 0-86568-049-3
Library of Congress No.: 83-50973

UP UNIQUE PUBLICATIONS
4201 VANOWEN PL., BURBANK, CA 91505

DISCLAIMER

Please note that the publisher of this instructional book is NOT RESPONSIBLE in any manner whatsoever for any injury which may occur by reading and/or following the instructions herein.

It is essential that before following any of the activities, physical or otherwise, herein described, the reader or readers should first consult his or her physician for advice on whether or not the reader should embark on the physical activity described herein. Since the physical activities described herein may be too sophisticated in nature, it is *essential that a physician be consulted*.

Dedication

To my wife, Cindy and our pride and joy in life,
our daughter, Jennifer Brooke.

Preface

Looking back at my martial arts career, I feel quite fortunate to have studied with some of the early karate legends. From Bill Wallace, I learned an advanced kicking system; from Joe Lewis I learned movement and from Joe Corley, I learned the missing ingredient that put it all together and enabled me to perform at my best—strategy. With the knowledge of how to devise different plans of strategy against different types of opponents, I gained the ability to exploit and turn my opponent's weaknesses into my advantage.

Experience was also a great teacher. During my career I fought some of the most talented and versatile point-fighters in the entire history of karate tournaments; Ray McCallum, Bobby Tucker, Mike Genova, Robert Harris, Nasty Anderson, Dan Anderson, Steve Fisher, Larry Kelly, John Longstreet, Al Francis, Jimmy Tabares, Alvin Prouder, and Eddie "Flash" Newman, to name a few. These fighters represent an exciting era of sports history in which I am proud to have participated.

In *Tournament Fighting*, I've compiled from my studies and experience, the drills, techniques and strategies that have suited my needs over the years. Although you may not have the same needs as I did, there is a wide range of practical information here to help you improve upon your own needs. But keep in mind that knowledge alone is not enough. To reach your fullest potential you must train with 100 percent effort. I wish you the best of luck.

Keith Vitali

Keith Vitali

Acknowlegements

I would like to thank all the kind people who assisted me in compiling this book; James Lew for participating in the photographs; Stuart Goldman for helping to put this book together; and to the excellent and cordial staff at Unique Publications headed by Curtis Wong.

I would like also to extend a special thanks to the many friends I made while competing in tournaments. It is because of their support that I've written this book; to Joe Corley and Larry Black for a prosperous partnership through the years; to Bobby Tucker for our good spirited rivalry which lasted through 20 matches; to my students for their loyalty and dedication; to Dan Anderson for his friendship and excellent book, *American Freestyle Karate;* to Mike Genova for his sense of humor and companionship during the traveling years; Mike Green for his leadership qualities and excellent attitude which have influenced my way of thinking; Pete Manchee, Steve Vitali, John Orch, Bill McCleod, Richard Jackson and the Genova Karate Studio who beat me into shape in the old days in Columbia, South Carolina; Joe Perone, Howard Jones, Jeff Farmer, Victor Green, Charles Fears, Robert Ray, Vernon Johnson and Gerald Howard, my workout gang in Atlanta; and finally to George Chung, John Chung and Karen Sheperd, a special group of people who put new life into form competition.

And lastly, to John Roper, from whom I received my black belt and who is responsible for developing my foundation with his emphasis on strong basics.

Table of Contents

- **9** Attitude and the Use of Imagery
- **15** Warm-Up and Flexibility Drills
- **25** Basic Training Drills
- **67** Intermediate Training Drills
- **99** Advanced (Angular) Training Drills
- **121** Timing and Distance Drills
- **131** Advanced Slow-Motion Kicking Drills
- **141** Flying Techniques
- **151** Questions and Answers in Strategy

Attitude and the Use of Imagery

TOURNAMENT FIGHTING

"In a business like major league baseball, most of us have similar athletic abilities. The differences are mental and emotional, and the big thing is mental preparation. That's where everything starts: the poise, the confidence, the concentration."

—Don Sutton, Dodgers Pitcher

In order to reach the top in any sport, you need not only the proper mechanics, form, and the ability to perform to your maximum level, but also a high degree of mental concentration and focus. This will allow you to project a sense of confidence that even your opponents will detect. The key to concentration is in establishing a mental point and maintaining it. In karate, when you have tuned your mental state to perfection, you will have an almost magical sense that you can score on anyone. You will be in tune with every rhythm in a match and can even sense what your opponent is going to throw before he throws it. "That's something called flow," explains Eric Soderholm, the former White Sox third baseman who is now a scout for the Cubs. "When you get into this flow, your concentration is so keen you actually feel you're the hitter. I could be at third base and be in such a good flow, so concentrated, that I could actually sense a ball was going to be hit to me."

How can you achieve this level of concentration? One method that I use in every aspect of life, from acting to karate, is that of *visualization*. The use of mental imagery to psych yourself up in sports is just now being studied as a science. The key here is to have a vivid imagination, so you can close your eyes and actually visualize what you want to happen. If you can visualize it, then you are that much closer to doing it.

When I want to improve my tennis game, I visualize the way Bjorn Borg hits a tennis ball. I close my eyes after seeing him destroy an opponent with his overpowering strokes, and imagine myself swinging a racket in the same manner. Every time I do this mental exercise I find that the first few games after I warm up are my best. When I begin to think about *how* I'm doing a particular stroke, I begin hitting home runs with my two-handed backhand. I've learned to just let go, and when I hit the ball, I imagine that it is actually Borg who is playing, not me.

I've used this mental exercise to aid my tournament fighting as well. Since the subconscious does not differentiate between what is fantasy and what has actually happened, you can store winning techniques in your mind simply by visualizing them. Here is the ritual I go through before each important tournament:

At a time when there are no distractions, such as driving a long distance or when I close my eyes before going to sleep (I sometimes add background music to help me really get into my fantasy), I actually go through the entire

ATTITUDE AND USE OF IMAGERY

tournament in my mind, from walking into the tournament site to hearing the applause after I win my imaginary match. I have a couple of people in mind whom I imagine might reach the finals, and I include them in my exercise.

In your visualization, it's important to feel everything, including touch, smell, and sound. Imagine walking out of the cold morning air into a warm gym, and feeling all the parts of your body warming up. Imagine going into the dressing room and begin psyching up as you slowly get in your combat attire. Then gear up with the necessary equipment, and imagine that you are feeling better than ever. As you walk out to the arena to do battle, feel everyone's eyes on you as you project a sense of confidence that even spectators in the stands can detect. If you haven't developed a so-called reputation yet, then laugh to yourself if no one is looking. Say to yourself, "They are all in for a big surprise today when I'm finished with them." Stay totally positive at all times.

As you begin to visualize the fight, imagine, if you like, that you and Bill Wallace are the same person, and go through the entire fight scoring at will. If I have someone in mind that I want to beat, I try to remember their particular fighting style, and figure out how to beat them.

To prepare for this type of exercise, I first watch the person I want to beat. I stand outside the ring and imagine that I am actually fighting him. I am totally honest, and call my own points. I react in my mind as if I am actually fighting. If he throws a backfist that I don't see, I give him the point in my mind. In my early fighting days, I would practice by going through every match this way. At the end of the match, I would tell myself what the actual score was. If I lost, I would smile and be pleased that I had given myself a practice round to fight this guy. Then I would formulate a strategy to beat him.

When you choose to visualize, go through these exercises another time. After you win your fight, imagine winning the tournament. Imagine the applause and the feeling of accomplishment as you pick up your trophy. If you believe that it can happen, it will.

Continue to use these positive thought patterns and visualizations when you're actually in a tournament situation. For example, when I set up a technique with which I want to score, I first see it land in my mind, and then execute it. If I don't score, then I turn it into a positive thought pattern instantly, telling myself my opponent was lucky that the techniques didn't get him. I honestly believe not only that my techniques will score, but that I will eventually go all the way to first place.

Arnold Palmer, the famous golf champion, was quoted as saying, "When I'm working well, I just don't think I'm going to miss a shot or a putt, and when I do, I'm surprised as hell. A golfer must think that way. He must say to

TOURNAMENT FIGHTING

the ball, 'Go to that hole.' The best players who ever played must have thought that way, willing the ball there, you see."

By focusing on confidence-producing thoughts and images, you can convert your losses into learning experiences that will ultimately make you a winner. Say you are fighting, and your opponent gets a point with a round kick to your head. Instead of thinking, "Now I'm behind and I'm losing," tell yourself, "Good, I've just learned my hands were down and now I'm going to correct that flaw in my defense." Tell yourself, "I'm the type of person who doesn't make the same mistake twice," and you will probably not make the same mistake. Now your defense is even stronger than it was, and this will be reflected in your projection of confidence, which is the greatest advantage in a fight. I believe that the best compliment given me throughout my career was not about how fast I was or how good my kicks looked, but that the confidence I displayed and the look I had made everyone think I was going to win. Your confidence is your greatest weapon.

Even if you have a poor outing at a tournament, you can turn that negative experience around and program it in a positive manner. I used to do this by honestly believing that when I lost I had learned something. When someone discovered a crack in my armor and penetrated my defense to win, I would smile to myself because what they actually did by defeating me was to give me the inspiration needed, the burning desire to go back to my studio and prepare for the next battle. When I lost a tournament, there was literally chaos in my sparring sessions as I trained for my next match. Vernon Johnson, a top national fighter, used to joke about this all the time. He used to kid me about seeing red in my eyes after I lost a tournament.

By practicing these exercises in visualization and keeping a positive attitude, you will eventually be able to sustain a high level of concentration through the tournament, whether you win or lose. Remember, however, that concentration does not mean tension. It's important not to psyche yourself out, or build up so much tension that you are as tight as a rubber band when you fight. I've found that fighters with an easy-going style who just have a good time often find themselves on the winners stand at the end of the tournament. The competitors who are able to loosen up before a match find that when the match actually begins, they are a good deal less tense and are able to concentrate on a higher level.

On the other hand, Ivan Lendel, a highly-ranked tennis player, does not care to be distracted from concentrating on his match by any means. He stays in his hotel room and doesn't take in the sights as he travels around the world. He feels that socializing and sightseeing distract him from what he is there to do, play tennis.

What works for one fighter may not work for another. The key, of course, is to find out what works best for you.

All of the mental techniques described in this chapter will help you

ATTITUDE AND USE OF IMAGERY

master the first step towards becoming a champion; believing in yourself. When you have the proper training and the right positive attitude, the only limit to your achievements are the ones you place on yourself. There is very little luck involved in becoming a winner—and you can make that luck happen.

Warm-Up and Flexibility Drills

Flexibility will give you not only your full range of motion, it will also allow you to study karate with less risk of pulling muscles. Stretching is the key to flexibility. But before you begin any stretching exercises, it's important to begin with an appropriate warm-up that will loosen up your body and warm the muscles by increasing your body heat. Some good warm-ups are jumping jacks, stationary bike riding, and jumping rope. Keep in mind that more injuries result from the lack of proper warm-up exercises than from action in sports.

When your body is sufficiently warmed-up for stretching, then I suggest you use the concentrated stretch method. This method concentrates on a particular group of muscles from a fixed position. Although many dance classes use a bounce stretching method which will eventually stretch you out, it places your muscles through much more shock than the concentrated stretch method. I have found that less injuries occur with this method.

When stretching, remember to stretch in a slow rhythmic pattern. Inhale as you prepare to stretch, exhale as you stretch. The more time and energy you put into stretching, the sooner you will gain flexibility.

Hamstring Stretch
Concentration: hamstring and lower back.

1) Stand with feet spread shoulder width.

WARM-UPS AND FLEXIBILITY DRILLS

2) Lower head to left knee and grab leg.

3) Shift to right knee and grab right leg.

4) Shift to the center and grab both ankles.

Advanced Hamstring Stretch

Concentration: hamstring, lower back and sides.

1) Stand with feet spread wider than shoulders.

2) Twist torso to right, bend forward and place left hand behind right ankle.

3) Twist under left arm and repeat exercises to the left side.

Chinese Split

Concentration: hamstring and groin.

1) Sit with feet extended to the sides.

2) Lean to the right. Head touches floor inside knee.

3) Repeat to the left side.

Chinese Splits cont.

4) Lean forward as far as possible.

American Split
Concentration: hamstring and groin.

1) Sit with legs extended and face left.

WARM-UPS AND FLEXIBILITY DRILLS

2) Lean forward and lower head to knee.

3) Sit with legs extended and face right.

4) Lean forward and lower head to knee.

Sitting Down Hamstring Stretch

Concentration: hamstring and hips.

1) Sit with left leg extended, right foot tucked in at left knee.

2) Keep your back straight. Lean to left knee and grab left foot. Repeat to the opposite side.

WARM-UPS AND FLEXIBILITY DRILLS

Advanced Sitting Down Hamstring Stretch
Concentration: hamstring and sides.

1) Sit with left leg extended, right foot tucked in at left knee, left hand on right knee.

2) Grab left foot with right hand.

3) Twist torso under right arm. Repeat to opposite side.

Basic Training Drills

The Reverse Punch

The general mechanics of the reverse punch taught in this basic chapter should be understood before attempting any of the punching drills outlined in this book.

When executing a reverse punch, it is important to understand that your potential for power is greatly increased as you incorporate your body weight with each punch.

First the weapon (reverse punch) begins towards its target; next the body follows as you pivot on your back foot. Remember to stay balanced as you punch and not to over-extend. Keep your non-punching hand high to block your head.

This same principle of body movement as an aid in power can also be seen in many different sports. Analogies can be drawn between a golfer's swing, a baseball batter's swing, and a boxer's punch. The key is to generate power by pivoting on the ball of your back foot and to utilize your legs, hips and shoulders, as well as your arms.

The Backfist

The backfist is said to be the quickest technique in competition. The speed of the backfist is generated by a quick recoil of the straight line technique. One tip is that you should think in terms of returning your backfist more quickly than you throw it.

Just as important as the actual delivery of the backfist is how you close the gap. Position your weight on the balls of your feet and have your lead hand in a high guard position rather than the low guard position. The lead hand in the high guard position is actually much closer to your opponent, therefore you should score more easily from this position. Next, incorporate movement of some kind to camouflage your initial move towards your opponent. It's much easier to detect movement from a stationary position than from a moving target.

Five Keys To A Winning Backfist

1. Stay poised on the balls of your feet.
2. Keep the lead hand in the guard position.
3. Incorporate either movement or deceptive feints before initiating the attack.
4. Thrust off of the back foot after the initial firing of your backfist.
5. Commit totally to the technique.

The Side Kick

All kicks have their special importance, but I believe the side kick is the key kick in any fighter's arsenal. Regardless of your physical size, a side kick, if developed properly, is a great aid to other techniques, can keep somebody off you, and can condition an opponent to drop his elbow. This reaction will render your other kicks more effective.

Keep in mind that not all top fighters have a backfist, or high hook kicks, but they *all* have the side kicks to repel formidable attacks.

The side kick can also be used to gain a psychological edge against an opponent. If you strike an opponent hard with a side kick, their conscious mind will try to stay positive; they'll tell themselves they're not worried about it. However, their unconscious mind has been *conditioned* by the pain from the first side kick and it will remember it for the rest of the match. Now when you chamber your leg in the same position that caused him pain earlier, his unconscious will take over and attempt to block it. This reaction will enable your other techniques to land more easily. I call this "conditioning" an opponent.

To prepare for a side kick, offensive or defensive, quickly raise the foot in a direct line between you and your opponent. This movement is the key, then thrust your kick in a straight line. Avoid raising your knee first and then shifting your hips. And remember, good form is essential to a side kick; if you have the timing and speed to catch somebody with it, but your form is no good, it's a wasted technique.

TOURNAMENT FIGHTING

Correct Method of Side Kick

1) Partners confront. Follow partner (right).

2) Slide left foot in a direct line between you and partner. Raise the foot in a straight line with the knee while chambering the leg. Step 3 from the incorrect method has been eliminated. This elimination cuts time but not power.

3) Execute a side kick.

Incorrect Method of Side Kick

1) Partners confront. Follow partner (right).

2) He slides and begins to lift his foot.

3) He raises his knee (his biggest mistake).

TOURNAMENT FIGHTING

Incorrect Method of a Side Kick cont.

4) By the time he pivots and turns, partner (left) strikes.

Side Kick Variation

(This is a quicker version of the side kick with emphasis of speed over power.)

1) Side stance.

BASIC TRAINING DRILLS

2) Slide up and pivot both knees slightly forward.

3) Chamber foot away from the body. This step is the major variation; leg isn't fully chambered.

4) Thrust kick.

Defensive Side Kick

Have your partner move quickly towards you and your strike. This drill will also improve your timing. Begin with 25 kicks on each leg and gradually work up to 100 kicks. Never back away from your charging partner.

1) Partners confront.

2) Partner (left) approaches.

BASIC TRAINING DRILLS

3) Chamber leg.

4) Thrust leg in straight line. Your body should not fall back after striking target. The power will recoil with you if it does.

Offensive Side Kick

1) Partners confront. Follow partner (right).

Offensive Side Kick cont.

2) Slide up and pivot toward target.

3) Chamber leg with knee close to body.

4) Thrust kick in a straight line.

BASIC TRAINING DRILLS

Slide Up Side Kick

1) Side stance.

2) Slide up and pivot.

3) Chamber leg in line with rear foot. Knee is slightly higher than foot which is as high as your rear.

Slide Up Side Kick cont.

4) Thrust your hip by rolling at a ¾ angle and kick slightly higher than your chambered foot to utilize the pushing muscles of your legs.

Backfist

1) Partners confront. Follow partner (right).

BASIC TRAINING DRILLS

2) Begin in a pivoted position. The fist moves first.

3) With body in a forward position, strike your opponent.

TOURNAMENT FIGHTING

Back Kick, Backfist

1) Partners confront. Follow partner (right).

2) Look over right shoulder, then rotate right.

3) Chamber right leg.

BASIC TRAINING DRILLS

4) Thrust leg.

5) Recoil leg and prepare for backfist.

6) Before falling into place, execute backfist.

TOURNAMENT FIGHTING

Backfist, Back Kick

1) Partners confront. Follow partner (right).

2) Step out with a backfist.

3) Look right, then rotate right as you pivot.

BASIC TRAINING DRILLS

4) Chamber right leg. Keep it closely tucked to body.

5) Thrust leg in a straight line.

TOURNAMENT FIGHTING

Reverse Punch

1) Forward fighting stance.

2) Reverse punch to the mid-section. The fist moves first and is followed by the turning of the body and hips at the end of the punch while pivoting on the ball of the rear foot. The guard hand is held high by the head for protection.

3) Side view of #1.

4) Side view of #2.

BASIC TRAINING DRILLS

Fake Middle Reverse Punch, Backfist

1) Partners confront. Follow partner (right).

2) Begin a middle reverse punch.

3) Before the reverse punch is fully extended, recoil it quickly and prepare for backfist.

Fake Middle Reverse Punch, Backfist cont.

4) Partner (left) is still fooled by the reverse punch, Backfist quickly.

Ridge Hand, Reverse Punch

1) Partners confront. Follow partner (right).

BASIC TRAINING DRILLS

2) Step out with a front ridge hand.

3) Begin pivoting.

4) Execute a high reverse punch.

Ridge Hand, Middle Reverse Punch

1) Partners confront. Follow partner (right).

2) Step out with front ridge hand.

3) Crouch, and . . .

BASIC TRAINING DRILLS

4) Reverse punch.

Backfist, Middle Reverse Punch

1) Partners confront. Follow partner (right).

2) Step out with a backfist.

3) Execute a reverse punch. Balance yourself properly and don't over-extend.

Hook Kick To Focus Pad

Your partner should hold target high. Work on gaining a full range of kicking, motion and concentrate on form.

1) Follow partner (right).

2) Slide up and chamber.

3) Execute kick.

Hook Kick to Focus Pad cont.

4) Extend leg upward and strike target.

Slide Up Backfist, Hook Kick

1) Partners confront. Follow partner (right).

BASIC TRAINING DRILLS

2) Step toward partner with back fist.

3) Slide up and pivot back foot.

4) Chamber right leg with foot outside partner's waist.

TOURNAMENT FIGHTING

Slide Up Backfist, Hook Kick cont.

5) Extend leg upward.

6) Bring foot back to partner's head. Weapon is either the heel or the bottom of the foot.

Front Kick

1) Partners confront. Follow partner (right).

2) Execute a high reverse punch.

3) Chamber back leg. Keep the body straight and knee at 90 degree angle.

Front Kick cont.

4) Thrust leg in a straight line.

Defensive Front Kick

1) Partners confront. Follow partner (right).

BASIC TRAINING DRILLS

2) As partner approaches, chamber your rear leg.

3) With your knee bent, make contact with target.

4) Utilizing your hips, thrust leg in a straight line.

TOURNAMENT FIGHTING

Power Kick

1) Partners confront. Follow partner (right).

2) Chamber back leg.

3) Utilizing hips, thrust leg in a straight line.

Slide Up Round Kick

1) Partners confront. Follow partner (right).

2) Slide up and pivot.

3) Raise right leg with knee aimed at partner. Stand as straight as possible. The more you lean, the less power you'll have. Again, 45 degree inclination is the norm.

Slide Up Round Kick cont.

4) Extend leg.

Back Leg Round Kick

1) Partners confront. Follow partner (left).

BASIC TRAINING DRILLS

2) Raise back leg 45 degrees behind you and begin to pivot on supporting foot.

3) Raise knee to a high chambered position.

4) Complete pivot with knee and foot striking target. When you kick, the power is generated from the turn of the hips.

Power Roundhouse Kick

1) Partners confront. Follow partner (left).

2) Pivot slightly on left foot as you begin to turn.

3) Chamber right leg at a 45 degree angle.

BASIC TRAINING DRILLS

4) Pivot and turn your hips as you strike target.

Swing Kick

1) Partners confront. Follow partner (right).

Swing Kick cont.

2) Slide up and pivot back foot.

3) Chamber leg for swing kick.

4) Snap swing kick to head.

BASIC TRAINING DRILLS

5) Knee and foot pass through target.

6) Foot drops.

Swing Kick, Round Kick

1) Partners confront. Follow partner (right).

2) Slide up and pivot back foot.

3) Chamber leg into swing position.

BASIC TRAINING DRILLS

4) Extend leg above target.

5) Recoil leg into round kick position.

6) Execute a round kick.

Intermediate Training Drills

TOURNAMENT FIGHTING

In this chapter I've outlined a series of drills that incorporate the basic drills into more intricate patterns and effective combinations. Here, emphasis is placed on the ability to hold your legs up and fire two or three kicks without dropping your leg.

Chambering Drill

This drill can develop the flexibility in your groin muscles and hips.

1) Lift leg into side kick position.

2) Pull leg back 45 degrees.

3) Chamber leg into hooking position by moving knee back and forth across center line.

INTERMEDIATE TRAINING DRILLS

Defensive Ridge Hand vs. Backfist

1) Partners confront. Follow partner (right).

2) As partner (left) steps out with offensive backfist, partner (right) parries with backfist.

3) Partner (right) pivots and executes a ridge hand.

TOURNAMENT FIGHTING

Counter Punch vs. Backfist

1) Partners confront. Follow partner (right).

2) As partner (left) executes a backfist, partner (right) shifts weight to rear leg and backs out of range.

3) Partner (right) then shifts weight forward and follows the recoil of partner (left) backfist.

INTERMEDIATE TRAINING DRILLS

4) Partner (right) executes a reverse punch.

Dash Punch

1) Partners confront. Follow partner (right).

TOURNAMENT FIGHTING

Dash Punch cont.

2) The weapon moves first.

3) Lunge across the center line with 100 percent commitment.

An additional dash punch drill: Have your partner take the arm nearest you and place it behind his back. Attempt to score your dash punch to the exposed section of his body before he can evade your attack. From this drill you'll learn to stop *telegraphing* your initial move when beginning an attack.

INTERMEDIATE TRAINING DRILLS

Round Kick, Side Kick

1) Partners confront. Follow partner (right).

2) Slide up and pivot.

3) Chamber leg in high round kick position.

Round Kick, Side Kick cont.

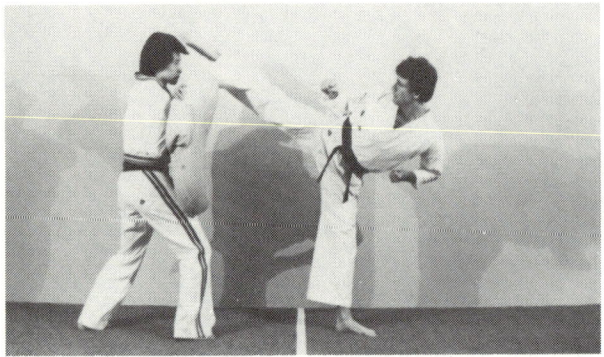

4) Deliver controlled round kick to head.

5) Chamber for side kick.

6) Thrust power side kick.

INTERMEDIATE TRAINING DRILLS

Side Kick, Round Kick

1) Partners confront. Follow partner (right).

2) Slide up as you pivot.

3) Chamber leg into side kick position.

Side Kick, Round Kick cont.

4) Deliver controlled side kick.

5) Chamber into high round kick position.

6) Strike target.

INTERMEDIATE TRAINING DRILLS

Pulling Round Kick, Back Fist

1) Partners confront. Follow partner (right).

2) Chamber a round kick.(For beginners only. The advanced fighter can combine 2 and 3.)

3) As you begin the execution of the round kick, let the forward momentum carry you across center line. Good form is important. Keep the body aligned as you're carried across the center line.

Pulling Round Kick, Backfist cont.

4) Complete the round kick.

5) Chamber round kick and prepare backfist.

6) Execute back fist.

INTERMEDIATE TRAINING DRILLS

Pulling Round Kick, Spinning Hook Kick

1) Partners confront. Follow partner (right).

2) Lift leg into round kick position.

3) Pull towards center line as you execute round kick.

TOURNAMENT FIGHTING

Pulling Round Kick, Spinning Hook Kick cont.

4) Drop leg and prepare to spin.

5) Look over right shoulder as you pivot.

6) Chamber into spinning hook kick position.

INTERMEDIATE TRAINING DRILLS

7) Extend leg.

8) Fold and hook leg back.

TOURNAMENT FIGHTING

Back Fist, Side Kick, Round Kick

1) Partners confront. Follow partner (right).

2) Step out with back fist as you . . .

3) Slide up and pivot.

INTERMEDIATE TRAINING DRILLS

4) Chamber leg for side kick.

5) Deliver side kick.

6) Recoil for round kick.

Back Fist, Side Kick, Round Kick cont.

7) Deliver round kick.

Back Fist, Round Kick, Side Kick

1) Partners confront. Follow partner (right).

INTERMEDIATE TRAINING DRILLS

2) Step out with back fist as you . . .

3) Slide up and pivot.

4) Chamber leg in round kick position.

Back Fist, Round Kick, Side Kick cont.

5) Deliver round kick.

6) Chamber round kick into side kick position.

7) Deliver side kick.

Back Fist, Double Side Kick

1) Partners confront. Follow partner (right).

2) Step out with back fist as you . . .

3) Slide up and pivot.

Back Fist, Double Side Kick cont.

4) Chamber leg for side kick.

5) Thrust side kick.

6) Recoil into side kick position.

INTERMEDIATE TRAINING DRILLS

7) Thrust side kick again.

Back Leg Round Kick, Side Kick

1) Partners confront. Follow partner (right).

Back Leg Round Kick, Side Kick cont.

2) Begin a back leg round kick.

3) Extend the round kick.

4) Recoil round kick.

INTERMEDIATE TRAINING DRILLS

5) Chamber leg into side kick position.

6) Deliver side kick.

TOURNAMENT FIGHTING

Back Fist, Double Round Kick

1) Partners confront. Follow partner (right).

2) Step out with back fist as you . . .

3) Slide up and pivot.

INTERMEDIATE TRAINING DRILLS

4) Chamber for round kick.

5) Deliver low round kick.

6) Recoil and chamber for high round kick.

Back Fist, Double Round Kick cont.

7) Deliver high round kick.

Back Fist, Round Kick, Side Kick, Round Kick

1) Partners confront. Follow partner (right).

INTERMEDIATE TRAINING DRILLS

2) Step out with back fist as you . . .

3) Slide up and pivot.

4) Chamber for high round kick.

Back Fist, Round Kick, Side Kick, Round Kick cont.

5) Deliver high round kick.

6) Chamber for side kick.

7) Deliver side kick.

INTERMEDIATE TRAINING DRILLS

8) Chamber for high round kick.

9) Deliver high round kick.

Advanced (Angular) Training Drills

TOURNAMENT FIGHTING

Angular footwork incorporates different angles to close the gap between you and your opponent. The techniques in this chapter utilize both defensive and offensive foot movement.

Defensively, I choose the round kick as the kick to angularly defend against because the circular motion of the kicking enables you to step away from the direction of the kick. I have found that the round kick is used more than any other kicking technique in a tournament.

Angular Backfist vs. Round Kick

1) Partners confront. Follow partner (right).

2) Partner slides up.

ADVANCED (ANGULAR) TRAINING DRILLS

3) As partner chambers for round kick, begin weapon (backfist) and movement with back foot.

4) Extend backfist while body is out of line from maximum impact point. Be sure to keep back hand up for protection.

TOURNAMENT FIGHTING

Angular Ridgehand vs. Round Kick

1) Partners confront. Follow partner (right).

2) Partner (left) slides up.

3) As partner (left) chambers for round kick, step out 45 degrees with left foot.

ADVANCED (ANGULAR) TRAINING DRILLS

4) Extend ridgehand.

Angular Reverse Punch vs. Round Kick

1) Partners confront. Follow partner (right).

Angular Reverse Punch vs. Round Kick cont.

2) Partner (left) slides up.

3) As partner (left) chambers for round kick, step out 45 degrees.

4) Extend reverse punch.

ADVANCED (ANGULAR) TRAINING DRILLS

Angular Rear Leg Hook vs. Round Kick

1) Partners confront. Follow partner (right).

2) Partner (left) slides up.

3) As partner (left) chambers for round kick, step out 45 degrees.

Angular Rear Leg Hook vs. Round Kick cont.

4) Chamber hook kick.

5) Execute kick. (Timing is essential here.)

ADVANCED (ANGULAR) TRAINING DRILLS

Angular Side Kick vs. Round Kick

1) Partners confront. Follow partner (right).

2) Partner (left) slides up.

3) As partner chambers for round kick, step out 45 degrees.

Angular Side Kick vs. Round Kick cont.

4) Chamber side kick.

5) Extend side kick.

ADVANCED (ANGULAR) TRAINING DRILLS

Angular Ridgehand, High Reverse Punch

1) Partners confront. Follow partner (right).

2) Step outside 45 degrees and begin ridge hand.

3) Execute a ridge hand to the midsection.

Angular Ridge Hand, High Reverse Punch cont.

4) Begin shifting body.

5) Rotate body and pivot.

6) Execute high reverse punch.

Angular Ridge Hand, Hook Kick

1) Partners confront. Follow partner (right).

2) Step out 45 degrees to outside.

3) Execute ridge hand to midsection (lowering his arms).

Angular Ridge Hand, Hook Kick cont.

4) Chambering rear leg hook kick.

5) Execute hook kick.

ADVANCED (ANGULAR) TRAINING DRILLS

Angular Rear Leg Side Kick

1) Partners confront. Follow partner (right).

2) Step 45 degrees to inside.

3) Chamber for side kick.

Angular Rear Leg Side Kick cont.

4) Extend the side kick.

Angular Rear Leg Hook Kick

1) Partners confront. Follow partner (right).

ADVANCED (ANGULAR) TRAINING DRILLS

2) Step 45 degrees to inside.

3) Chamber back leg for hook kick.

4) Execute hook kick.

Angular Rear Leg Side Kick, Round Kick

1) Partners confront. Follow partner (right).

2) Step to inside 45 degrees.

3) Chamber side kick.

ADVANCED (ANGULAR) TRAINING DRILLS

4) Execute side kick.

5) Pull back 45 degrees and chamber for round kick.

6) Execute round kick.

TOURNAMENT FIGHTING

Angular Ridge Hand vs. Hook Kick

1) Partners confront. Follow partner (right).

2) Partner (left) slides up.

3) As partner (left) chambers hook kick, step out 45 degrees to outside.

ADVANCED (ANGULAR) TRAINING DRILLS

4) Execute ridge hand.

Timing and Distance Drills

TOURNAMENT FIGHTING

Professional baseball pitchers understand timing as well as any professional in sports. Very few pitchers have the velocity behind a pitch to consistently overpower a hitter. Even Nolan Ryan, a ball player with a 100 m.p.h.-plus fast ball uses an off speed pitch that keeps batters guessing; Will it come at 50 m.p.h. or 105 m.p.h? Speed isn't enough. When a pitcher continually throws pitches at the same velocity, it doesn't take long for a batter to adjust to the speed. Fernando Valenzuela, one of the most effective pitchers in the pro ranks today can't even pitch the 90 m.p.h. speed, but he has effective timing.

The same principles of speed and timing are also true for karate fighters. The ability to execute fast kicks is no guarantee that the kicks will be effective. In tournaments I have purposely thrown a series of kicks at a slow continuous speed to condition an opponent's response and expectations, then zapped him with a quick kick. Quickly chambering your leg and pausing can also disrupt an opponent's blocking rhythm if you condition him with three or four consecutive kicks. Perfect timing (knowing when to kick) is a greater asset than having great speed.

Distance is also correlated with timing. I've outlined a few drills here that will help you to better understand timing and distance.

Lateral Movement From A Defensive Side Kick

1) Partners confront. Follow partner (right).

TIMING AND DISTANCE DRILLS

2) Partner (left) chambers for side kick.

3) As partner thrusts side kick, move in a lateral motion to the inside of the kick.

TOURNAMENT FIGHTING

Avoiding Attack

1) Partners confront. Follow partner (right).

2) Partner (left) chambers for side kick.

3) As he thrusts, back out of the way by leaning on back leg and staying as close to the attacking foot as possible. This keeps you in range for a counter technique.

TIMING AND DISTANCE DRILLS

Back Fist Timing Drill

1) Partners confront. Follow partner (right).

2) Partner (left) steps forward across center line and . . .

3) Slides up.

Back Fist Timing Drill cont.

4) As partner (left) chambers for side kick, reach out with front hand and lightly touch his head. Keep back hand open to protect the ribs.

Evasive Angular Movement vs. Side Kick

1) Partners confront. Follow partner (right).

TIMING AND DISTANCE DRILLS

2) Partner (left) slides up and . . .

3) Chambers.

4) Step to inside of side kick. You are still in range to score with hands or feet.

TOURNAMENT FIGHTING

Avoiding Side Kick With Back Leg

1) Partners confront. Follow partner (right).

2) Partner (left) slides up.

3) As partner (left) chambers, begin movement with back foot.

TIMING AND DISTANCE DRILLS

4) Step to the inside to avoid impact.

Advanced Slow-Motion Kicking Drills

TOURNAMENT FIGHTING

Through flexibility and stretching you create the ability to kick at close range. You'll need flexibility to accomplish the slow motion drills in this chapter. These drills also improve kicking at close angle distances. Very few people fear kicks in the head when there is no gap between the fighters. These drills will make you a kicking threat even at close range.

Foot To Foot: Side Kick Variation

Stay as close to your partner as possible. Form is critical. Any deviation detracts from form.

1) Partners stand foot to foot. Follow partner (right).

2) Lift side kick straight up.

ADVANCED SLOW MOTION KICKING DRILLS

3) Aim at partner's head. The body is inclined at no more than a 45 degree angle.

Roundhouse Kick Variation

Control and emphasis on good posture are important. Correct body inclination is crucial. Bend only from your sides and not at the stomach. A rule of thumb to follow is the higher your body and head position, the stronger your kick. And when you're upright, you can use your hands too.

1) Partners stand foot to foot. Follow partner (right).

Roundhouse Kick Variation cont.

2) Pivot rear foot from a 45 degree to a 90 degree angle and raise the knee as high as possible.

3) Extend leg to head.

Hook Kick Variation
Stay as close to partner as possible.

1) Partners stand foot to foot. Follow partner (right).

2) Raise knee as high as possible.

3) Extend leg in front of partner's head.

TOURNAMENT FIGHTING

Shoulder To Shoulder

In the shoulder to shoulder range, the closeness adds difficulty to the stretch. Don't step out. Lean back as little as possible.

Roundhouse Variation

1) Partners stand shoulder to shoulder.

2) Raise knee.

ADVANCED SLOW MOTION KICKING DRILLS

3) Lean back as little as possible and extend foot high.

Hook Kick Variation

1) Partners stand shoulder to shoulder.

Hook Kick Variation cont.

2) Turn hip, raise knee, and chamber foot.

3) Extend leg in front of partner's head.

4) Hook kick back toward partner's head.

ADVANCED SLOW MOTION KICKING DRILLS

Flying Techniques

TOURNAMENT FIGHTING

Flying kicks increase the range of your weapon with sufficient power. The key is not to allow your trailing leg to get too high off the ground, but to extend both legs into an aerial split. The most dangerous point in using aerial techniques is not during the kick, but on the way down after the kick has been executed.

There is a high degree of risk in mastering these aerial techniques; this basically accounts for the lack of their use in point-sparring. But once learned properly, they can be used quite effectively.

Jump Spinning Swing Kick

1) Partners confront. Follow partner (right).

2) Jump with both feet simultaneously. Chamber into hook kick position.

FLYING TECHNIQUES

3) Execute spinning swing kick.

Flying Angular Back Leg Side Kick

1) Partners confront. Follow partner (right).

Flying Angular Back Leg Side Kick cont.

2) Step out 45 degrees.

3) Jump off left foot and chamber to side kick position.

4) Cock the back leg.

FLYING TECHNIQUES

5) Execute side kick.

Jump Away Side Kick

1) Partners confront. Follow partner (right).

Jump Away Side Kick cont.

2) As partner (left) attacks, step back or away.

3) Prepare to jump.

4) Jump and chamber to side kick position.

FLYING TECHNIQUES

5) Execute side kick.

Jump Hook Kick

1) Partners confront. Follow partner (right).

Jump Hook Kick cont.

2) Jump with both legs, and chamber right leg into hook kick position.

3) Deliver hook kick.

FLYING TECHNIQUES

Jump Spinning Crescent Kick

1) Partners confront. Follow partner (right).

2) Jump and chamber leg into crescent kick position.

3) Execute a crescent kick.

Questions and Answers in Strategy

TOURNAMENT FIGHTING

I've formulated this chapter from the most frequently asked questions in my schools and seminars. I offer answers that have proven successful for me and many others I've worked with. I hope they work for you.

WHAT'S THE BEST STYLE A TOURNAMENT FIGHTER CAN STUDY?

Style doesn't mean as much as the person in the style. If you wish to advance in the martial arts, you should develop your own fighting style. You must incorporate knowledge from many different systems if you are truly to succeed in the martial arts.

I received my black belt in tae kwon do, but have been influenced by many styles. I've studied with Presas, Master in arnis, exchanged ideas with Mike Genova and Dan Andersen of American karate, Bill Wallace, who's got a Japanese/Okinawan background, and Jeff Smith and Joe Corley, both of whom have Korean backgrounds. I've also studied kung-fu. So the answer is, study as many styles as possible and take what works for you out of each one.

AREN'T WE DESTROYING ANCIENT MARTIAL ARTS SYSTEMS WHEN WE TRY TO IMPROVE WHAT THE MASTERS HAVE TAUGHT US?

No! Because we can trace karate to ancient times should we continue to teach in old fashioned ways? This is ridiculous.

The tournament scene today is still relatively new. It needs those who will take the initiative to develop new ways of teaching and new theories. It's the innovators who wind up achieving success, because they're not stuck imitating old techniques.

HOW DO I LEARN KICKING SPEED?

Some people maintain the position that either you are born with slow "twitch" muscles or fast "twitch" muscles and that speed can't be improved. Forget this.

Though you might not have the physical abilities to outkick Bill Wallace, there is always room for improvement. Compare the times you've kicked when you weren't in the best of physical condition to those times you were in top shape. Surely you must recall some difference in raw speed.

Repetition kicks in the air (no resistance) are a good way to increase speed. By emphasizing a quick recoil, quick results can occur.

QUESTIONS AND ANSWERS IN STRATEGY

Based upon a theory that states repetition increases efficiency, I've come up with the 1000-plus kicking drill. The 1000-plus kicking drill is broken down into three phases. Use moderation with each phase until you feel comfortable, then progress to the next phase. With a partner, you can complete this drill in 45 minutes. Alternate each kick with your partner and emphasize the snap (recoil), form and focus. You'll get from this drill what you put into it so give 100 percent. And enjoy it!

And if you favor different kicks than the ones I've prescribed from my regimen, substitute your own kicks in their place.

Phase 1: Single Kicks

DRILL	REPS PER LEG	TOTAL KICKS, BOTH LEGS
1. front kick	15	30
2. side kick	15	30
3. front leg round kick	15	30
4. back leg round kick	15	30
5. hook or swing kick	15	30
6. back kick	15	30
		TOTAL KICKS 180

Phase 2: Double Kicks

DRILL	REPS PER LEG (2 KICKS PER REP)	TOTAL KICKS, BOTH LEGS
1. side kick, round kick	15	60
2. front round kick, side kick	15	60
3. swing (hook), round kick	15	60
4. front kick, round kick	15	60
5. round kick, round kick	15	60
		TOTAL KICKS 300

STATIONARY ROUND KICK

Both partners take same side, (left to left or right to right). Partners keep each other stationary by holding hands. This should ease concern for balance. Now lift the knee as high as possible and throw 50 round kicks. Repeat with the other leg.

REPS PER LEG
50
TOTAL KICKS, BOTH LEGS
100

ROUND KICKS

Continuing from the last drill, partners release hands. Concentration on balance is now required. Keep the knee as high as possible and throw 50 round kicks. Repeat with the other leg.

REPS PER LEG
50
TOTAL KICKS, BOTH LEGS
100
TOTAL KICKS, PHASE 2 500

Phase 3

DRILL	REPS PER LEG (3 KICKS PER REP)	TOTAL KICKS BOTH LEGS
1. round kick, round kick, round kick	15	90
2. side kick, round kick, side kick	15	90
3. round kick, side kick, round kick	15	90
4. round kicks without holding hands	50 kicks per leg	100

QUESTIONS AND ANSWERS IN STRATEGY

TOTAL KICKS PHASE 3	370
TOTAL KICKS PHASE 1	180
PHASE 2	500
PHASE 3	370
	1050

HOW DO I LEARN TO KICK HARDER?

There are many exercises that will strengthen your legs. Running or lifting leg weights are fine methods. But for quicker results, kick air shields, or some sort of heavy bag. Pad-kicking for power is also a good method.

WHEN I FIGHT WITH MY STRONG LEG FORWARD, MY WEAK HAND IS THE ONE I HAVE TO PUNCH WITH. WHAT CAN I DO TO CORRECT THIS SITUATION?

Although some people are equally effective with both hands and legs, this is not the norm. Most people favor one side, hand, and leg.

With this limitation, your strong leg forward with a reverse punch from the opposite hand is one of the most effective combinations. You can be confident with it.

The trouble with placing a strong leg forward (where your ridge hand and backfist might be effective,) is that you have to use your weaker hand for your power punch.

The best way to strengthen that weaker hand is to work with it on a heavy bag. Once you gain confidence with that weaker hand, when an opponent steps inside your stronger leg you won't be at his mercy.

IS WEIGHT TRAINING ADVISABLE FOR MARTIAL ARTISTS?

The old "muscle bound" athlete who didn't understand how to control his diet ran into the problem of having a layer of fat next to the muscles and bones. This restricted movement.

Today, through a better understanding of kinesology, athletes can develop muscles and reduce fat. This allows for a greater range of motion with strength. Therefore, weight training is advisable when done properly. The Nautilus method, where flexibility is emphasized along with muscle development, is an excellent system. Stretching before and after lifing weights is advised.

ALTHOUGH I'M INVOLVED IN A VIGOROUS TRAINING PROGRAM, I'M NOT FIGHTING ANY BETTER. WHAT CAN THE PROBLEM BE?

In point karate, I've encountered many people who place more importance on their endurance training than on the actual fighting itself. Running, swimming, kicking heavy bags, punching speed bags and jumping rope will only get you into good physical shape. If you want to be a good fighter, you must practice wisely and incorporate proper training drills that will sharpen your techniques. Then you must free spar often. The more you free spar in the studio, the better studio fighter you'll become; the more tournaments you fight in, the better tournament fighter you'll become.

I HAVE SPEED, POWER AND VERSATILE TECHNIQUES. WHY CAN'T I SCORE?

All the necessary ingredients in the world won't help you if you don't have timing.

There's a world of difference between *knowing how-to* and *knowing when-to*.

To initiate a program that'll develop your sense of timing, start with rhythm kicking drills. Here's a drill that works well for beginners; Working with a partner, have him slowly throw a backfist at you. Every time he lifts his elbow for the backfist, throw a focused defensive side kick from a side stance. Your partner should gradually increase his speed until eventually he is moving at his top speed. You must keep your side kick up to speed with his backfist. In a short time the side kick will become reflexive.

Try alternating kicks with a partner. As he recoils, you kick, and as you recoil, he kicks. This should develop rhythm in your movements. Don't break the rhythm.

Have your partner throw a front leg, round kick at you. As he raises to kick, begin a spinning hook or spinning back kick. The key here is not to block, but to spin at the correct moment (when he begins to chamber the kick). You can incorporate this timing format with many different combinations of kicks and punches.

QUESTIONS AND ANSWERS IN STRATEGY

AS I LEARN NEW TECHNIQUES, HOW CAN I IMPLEMENT THEM INTO MY FIGHTING ARSENAL WITHOUT PAYING FOR IT PHYSICALLY?

A method I use extensively in my schools is *circle kicking*. This exercise involves two or more partners. Partners form a circle. Partner 1 executes his technique toward a partner next to him, 2. Partner 2 blocks but doesn't counter. Partner 2 then executes his technique to the next partner. Go around the circle in this manner. This method allows everyone a chance to see how others execute techniques and to try their own without having to eat a side kick during the learning process.

After you feel comfortable with your new techniques and moves, try them out with confidence when you spar.

SHOULD I PRACTICE FAKING AS I WOULD ANY OTHER TECHNIQUE?

Faking should be practiced as a separate drill. Practice faking with arms, head, shoulders, hips, knees and with different kicks and punches.

When faking with a front hand technique such as a backfist, make your fakes as realistic as possible. If your opponent doesn't react, then you haven't sold him on the idea that you can score with that technique.

A faking strategy I used for years was to begin a match by immediately scoring a backfist. The next time I'd throw a backfist, I'd get an immediate reaction from my opponent because his response was conditioned from the first successful score against him. His unconscious mind would store this information and trigger an instinctive block every time he's see a backfist. I'd then use this reaction to land a different technique.

Imagine somebody kicking you in the groin with a front kick. The next time you see that leg chambering for a front kick, even if you detect it might be a fake, you will automatically block your groin because you've been conditioned.

Faking to set up a real technique with which to score is an *indirect attack*. A *direct attack* is employing singular movements towards your opponent.

IS IT BETTER TO MOVE OR STAND?

Movement is extremely important. I remember when boxers were first upset with Muhammad Ali because he wouldn't stand still long enough for anybody to hit him. His movement frustrated opponents and got them to open up their defense for his counter.

Your physical size and who you're fighting should determine the amount of movement. For example, if you have a heavyweight coming at you and you're a super lightweight then movement is essential.

Early in my career I learned a valuable lesson from Joe Lewis. In a seminar, I tried to kick him. He was never in a set stance. He would move back, to the side, or at me. Movement was taboo in the early '70's. "Stand your ground and get beaten like a man" was the school of thought in those days. Lewis's movement was revolutionary. It was what I was searching for. And when the world heavyweight champion in full-contact told me it was OK to move, I threw away all the traditional downward and inside blocks. It was from Lewis I learned that when you remain stationary and engage in the blocking and parrying game, you are usually playing right into someone's game plan.

SHOULD I FIGHT FROM ONLY ONE SIDE?

Some instructors teach their students to fight with their strong side forward. Some great fighters, such as Bill Wallace, favor one side in competition.

Imagine you are facing one of these fighters in a match and you know they are potentially dangerous with one leg. Now, imagine that you accidentally slip and ram your knee into his one good leg. He is now only a puncher, whereas if he were adept with both legs, he could change sides.

One of my first goals as a fighter was to achieve the ability to fight with either side. And with hard work I reached this goal. But before I did, when somebody I was fighting would change to the side on which I wasn't effective, I would panic. I was limited.

When you don't mind an opponent fighting from either side forward, and you feel comfortable with both of yours, then you are on your way to becoming a better fighter.

SHOULD I HAVE A PRE-FIGHT STRATEGY AND ATTEMPT TO SET UP AN OPPONENT FOR A FAVORITE TECHNIQUE OR SHOULD I FIGHT WITH MY NATURAL ABILITY AND ATTEMPT TO SCORE WHEN I SEE AN OPENING?

Experience will teach you your limitations and abilities. Many experienced fighters have a certain strategy, a game plan on how to score. From fighting

QUESTIONS AND ANSWERS IN STRATEGY

in numerous tournaments, they've gained the experience and ability to take advantage of the opportunity as it presents itself.

I've known only one fighter who relied totally on his reflexes, and that was one of the nation's top then lightweights in the 70's, Bobby Tucker. He could use this approach because he was an extremely quick fighter.

IS THERE AN ADVANTAGE TO INITIATING THE ATTACK?

Yes. Fighers who initiate the attack first also seem to score at a higher rate than those who wait. The reason is simple. Imagine two fighters of equal ability in a ring. One fighter begins his attack. The judges will focus their attention on the moving fighter. With the judges attention on him, he begins to cross the gap. He has the judges watching his every move. Then the other fighter makes a move, but the judge's focus is still on the first fighter. This, or course, is to your advantage.

HOW SHOULD I CLOSE THE GAP WHEN I FIGHT?

You may flirt with the critical distance point by crossing the gap with a fake backfist, jab, or kick, but don't cross it unless you do so with 100 percent commitment.

If you encounter an effective kick, I suggest beginning with a round, side, or front kick to force the opponent to block kicks and leave an opening for your punches. This is especially useful when fighting a side kick.

If you want to close the gap with a backfist, try faking a forward stance with your rear leg as if you were in a starting position for a race. Lead with your weapon (backfist) and thrust off of your back leg. Commit yourself fully.

SHOULD KARATE FIGHTERS INCORPORATE MORE KICKS THAN PUNCHES OR MORE PUNCHES THAN KICKS?

Karate fighting works best when you have an even ratio of punches to kicks. Your feet set up your hands and your hands set up your feet. It's difficult to excel without this combination.

TOURNAMENT FIGHTING

HOW DO I KNOW IF I'M FIGHTING A PUNCHER OR A KICKER?

The first thing you can do if you've never seen your opponent fight before is to make a quick fake and watch for his response. Does he instinctively pick up a leg for a defensive kick or does he widen his stance and prepare to battle it out with his hands? His reaction to your fake should reveal the answer. With much practice and experience, you can learn to identify your opponent as a puncher or kicker with only one fake.

IS THERE A PARTICULAR THEORY THAT YOU'VE FOUND BENEFICIAL IN SPARRING WITH MANY DIFFERENT TYPES OF FIGHTERS?

Basically, the universal strategy for fighting is to be better at your strong points than your opponent. For example, if you are predominantly better at the punching game, utilize this strong point (punching) to score.

Have you ever noticed why good kickers are seldom scored on by kicks and good punchers are seldom scored on by punches? This is because each fighter understands what it is they rely upon most. Thus the kicker studies every aspect of the kicking game. Through many repetitious kicks, a kicker has analysed everything there is to know about kicking. So when an opponent chambers a kick, a kicker reads it instantly and can react in time without being scored on. Precise punching works best against kickers.

The same principle is true for the puncher. Punchers develop every aspect of punching and when an opponent initiates an attack with a punch, a puncher reads him like a book. Deceptive kicks work best on punchers.

Remember that some fighters pose the double threat of being extremely knowledgeable in both areas, but most fighters usually favor one over the other.

HOW DO I FIGHT SOMEBODY WHO IS TOTALLY DEFENSIVE AND CONTINUALLY THROWS DEFENSIVE SIDE KICKS?

A typical answer to this question is "be better and quicker at your attack than he is at his defense." But problems arise when you fight somebody with more skill in their field than you have in yours. One strategy is to close the gap with your kicks and force him to block.

I've used another strategy quite often. Keeping in mind that a fighter who exhibits these defensive traits does so because of habit, you can trick him

QUESTIONS AND ANSWERS IN STRATEGY

out of his defensive shell to the offense at which he probably isn't as good. Now you have him fighting in a style unaccustomed to him, and bingo!—he's yours.

DO YOU HAVE SPECIFIC TRAINING DRILLS TO IMPROVE MY PUNCHING?

Yes. Try these:
1) Dash punch with partner:
Have your partner place his front arm behind him, exposing his scoring area to you. The idea is to stand at normal fighting distance and attempt to land a dash punch to the open area before your partner can back up and avoid attack. It is important to have your partner give positive feedback to let you know if you are telegraphing your initial movements. Make sure that your dash punch moves first, independent of the rest of your body. Then your body follows through. In a short time, with the help of your partner, you will be able to explode off the line and beat your opponent's defense with this drill. As you begin this exercise, be sure you're in a proper forward fighting stance with weight on the ball of your feet, then thrust by pushing off your back leg for the quickest movement across the gap.
2) Dash punch with target:
Have your partner hold a small focus pad at head level as you stand at normal fighting distance. Here, you are trying to strike the target with a dash punch before your partner can react by moving the target up or down to avoid your strike. Again feedback from your partner is suggested for best results.
3) Reverse (straight) punch with a target:
Have your partner hold a small focus pad at head level as you stand at normal fighting distance. Your partner simply drops the target as you attempt to strike it before the target hits the ground. This drill will improve your reaction timing with your punches.

HOW DO I FIGHT A TOTALLY OFFENSIVE FIGHTER?

A logical answer is to develop a superior defense against their offense. You can achieve this with defensive side kick drills: 1) For power, defensive side kick against a charging partner holding pads. 2) Defensive side kick against partner's backfist. Have partner start slowly with backfist, then gradually pick up speed.

TOURNAMENT FIGHTING

Another method might be to get an offensive fighter who probably trains in this manner to go on the defense. Go right at him and make him fight defensively. It's easier said than done, but it works.

HOW DO I FIGHT A RUNNER?

Cutting off the ring and using sweeps tends to slow a runner down. As you chase him, a runner's best weapon is the defensive backfist or jump away side kick. So be on the lookout and keep the pressure on.

WHAT CAN I DO AGAINST A SKILLED JUMP AWAY SIDE KICK?

I would suggest using the following strategies: As you attack and your opponent is in mid-air with his jump away side kick, sweep his hanging leg with your front or back leg.

I developed an effective jump side kick early in my career because of my height. In the pre-gear days, I was usually in the heavyweight division. Weighing 150 pounds, I found myself being overpowered by much heavier fighters. Even when I scored, they made sure I paid for it. So I developed a kick I could execute on the run. Later, after many seminars where I taught this technique, and traveling the U.S. on the tournament circuit, I found fighters using this same technique against me.

The next step was to devise a sweep that could counter this move. Once you counter, an opponent will keep both his feet planted on the ground for the remaining portion of the fight.

The second strategy is simply to corner the jumper close to a boundary line, fake hard at him and watch him fly out of the ring to get penalized for running out of bounds.

HOW DO I FIGHT A BLOCKER, JAMMER-TYPE OF FIGHTER?

I call this type of fighter a target. Against a target who likes to jam kicks, I suggest initiating multiple kicks. Targets are easy to fight because when they block and jam your kicks they're playing right into your plan. You'll always know where they'll be when you attack.

Also you can fake kicks to one side of the body and then quickly shift to the other side. For example, a round kick, side kick combination works extremely well. The possible combinations against a target are limitless.

QUESTIONS AND ANSWERS IN STRATEGY

HOW DO I FIGHT AGAINST A PUNCHER?

I recommend movement to get a puncher to open up and over extend. Remember, punchers understand the punching game; it's what they spend most of their time practicing. Develop a deceptive attack if you intend to use your hands against an effective puncher.

HOW DO I FIGHT AGAINST A KICKER?

I believe groin kicks are the best weapon to use against them. Attacks to the groin tend to keep their feet down. After this type of threat, a good kicker fears even the puncher, not just another good kicker.

HOW DO I FIGHT A COUNTER TYPE FIGHTER?

This type fighter either blocks or barely backs up and then counters. Against counter punches, multiple kicks work well. Chambering a favorite round kick and quickly switching to a side kick without putting the foot down is a good technique. Everyone loves to throw a round kick. It's the easiest to block because of its circular pattern. Tempt the counter fighter with the round kick and surprise him with the side kick.

HOW DO I FIGHT A COMBINATION FIGHTER?

This is the hardest fighter to fight. Punches and kicks coming at you in combinations make defense difficult. But even these fighters have flaws. They have openings and cracks in their defense. Capitalize upon their openings with timed techniques.
Erratic fakes are also a good way to disturb their smooth combinations.

HOW DO I FIGHT A SWEEPER?

I've found that lifting the front foot up for sweeps against the front leg works well. You can also counter with a side, round or hook kick. For sweeps again the back leg, going on the offense at the earliest detection of the sweep can be quite effective. A reverse punch or backfist also works well here.

TOURNAMENT FIGHTING

HOW DO I FIGHT A TALLER AND HEAVIER OPPONENT?

Remember, it's not the size of the dog in the fight that counts; it's the size of the fight in the dog.

Of course, a larger opponent has the advantage in reach and size, but with a quick deduction of his weak points, you can devise a game plan to win.

To analyze the larger opponent, first fake toward him with a punch or kick. His reaction will indicate the type of fighter you are matched against. Then check his speed. Does his size hinder his ability to stop your blitz? Is he in a defensive stance with more weight on his back leg, or is he in a forward fighting stance with his feet not in a straight line? Does he chamber his side kick properly? Could he effectively use it to repel an attack?

I could go on and on, but the idea is to quickly analyze and implement a strategy to win. Play off their weaknesses.

A possible solution for entry into a larger opponent's defense is to follow the recoil of his kicks.

Or set him up. Condition the opponent by backing up twice, each time a little deeper than before. The third time he attacks he'll attempt to make up the distance by stepping out with his front foot. Attack him as his back foot slides up in preparation for a kick.

From these few examples, you can see that strategies *are* possible even against larger opponents.

HOW DO I FIGHT SOMEBODY SMALLER THAN ME?

Usually a smaller opponent is quicker than his adversary and a strategy that will negate his speed advantage is needed. Again, as with facing any opponent, analyze his abilities as a fighter and use your physical advantages to score. Keep him outside of your range.

An effective strategy against somebody smaller is to try and take the fight out of him. For example, set him up by throwing a low round kick and forcing him to block. You may now use your reach advantage for a lunging backfist.

Or try to use your height advantage by standing as high as possible in your fighting stance. As long as you are mobile and balanced, you can even stand out of a semi-stance. It will frustrate the smaller fighter attempting to score kicks on a target he can't reach. If you lower yourself to the height of the smaller opponent, then you negate your height advantage.

QUESTIONS AND ANSWERS IN STRATEGY

HOW DO I FIGHT SOMEONE WHO IS FASTER THAN I AM?

A specific strategy is needed when dealing with someone who is faster than you. I strongly urge you not to be a stationary fighter since this will benefit your partner by knowing exactly where you will be as he charges. Circular movement would be one recommendation with the strategy of attempting to force your quicker adversary into over-extending in his assault towards you.

Another strategy might be to take the fight to him using deceptive kicks such as a round kick, side kick combination.

IF I'M AHEAD 2-0 IN A "FIRST TO 3" POINT MATCH, SHOULD I GO FOR THE THIRD POINT OR ATTEMPT TO RUN OUT THE CLOCK?

Time after time I've seen fighters take control of a fight and have a 2-0 lead on their opponent and this question of "now what should I do?" is written all over their face. By the time they have figured out what to do the score is 2-2 and they are now fighting with the momentum in their opponent's field.

Under most circumstances I would suggest going after the last point while you are controlling the ring and have the momentum in your favor.

One particular match comes to mind. I was fighting Bobby Tucker in the finals. After the first two confrontations in the match I was down 2-0 because of Bobby Tucker's overpowering speed factor. I was standing still trying to beat him to the punch and he was just too fast. At that precise moment all I could think of at first was that he was too quick, when I noticed Bobby was standing still with a blank look on his face. I immediately threw a backfist and scored. Again the same look was present and again I scored with a backfist. Now the score was 2-2 and before Bobby could regain control of the match I threw another backfist and won the match. Afterwards, Tucker told me that after he had me 2-0 he started thinking, "Should I get my third point or let the time run out?" By the time he could figure it out I was already in control of the match.

Therefore remember this strategy; when you are down 2-0 take the fight to them.

HOW DO YOU FIGHT AGAINST AN OVERPOWERING-BLITZ TYPE OF FIGHTER WHO IS GOOD AT COMBINING BOTH KICKS AND PUNCHES?

I recommend you control the tempo in the ring by incorporating fakes to break up their timing, making it difficult for them to set up an attack. By forcing the action in the ring (such as initiating the attack with kicks) you force the opponent to block as you score with punches. If you remain stationary and let them strike first then you are playing into their game plan.

HOW DO YOU FIGHT A PERSON WHO HAS A GOOD DEFENSE AND CONTINUOUSLY THROWS RIDGE HANDS?

Attempt to set your opponent up rather than challenging him with a direct attack. If you attack to beat him to the punch; then you are trying to beat him at what he does best. It won't work.

Set your opponent up with a backfist for one strategy and as he counters with a ridge hand, then you've set him up for any one of your favorite techniques to the mid-section.

WHAT IS THE BEST WAY TO WARM UP IN A TOURNAMENT BEFORE I START FIGHTING?

I usually begin my warm-up procedure about one hour before I go into the ring. I begin by stretching. After I feel loose I gear up and get with a partner to exchange kicks back and forth for about 15 minutes. I stretch again and prepare mentally for my competition. Then I light spar with about 2 to 4 different people at the tournament (from different weight divisions) to tune up properly.

Basically you need to discover what is suitable to your needs, but I recommend breaking a good sweat before competition.

THE WEEK BEFORE A BIG TOURNAMENT HOW WOULD YOU TRAIN?

Monday: Work on power kicks against pads and air shields. A cardiovascular type workout with emphasis on conditioning, followed by sparring.

Tuesday: Drills such as those emphasized in this book, double kicks, etc. Speed emphasized rather than sparring.

Wednesday: Work on strategy and heavy night of sparring.

Thursday: Timing drills only—polish my techniques up. No sparring unless I feel I need it.

Friday: Rest. In order to "peak" on Saturday you *must* have rest.

Saturday: Tournament.

QUESTIONS AND ANSWERS IN STRATEGY

IT SEEMS THAT THE BEST FIGHTERS ARE VERY DECEPTIVE IN THEIR ATTACKS. HOW CAN I LEARN TO BE DECEPTIVE?

By incorporating deceptive movement drills in your training regime. Remember, sparring is only a game, so enjoy yourself; experiment with deception techniques, such as faking low to the groin and then backfisting high.

When trying to be deceptive in closing the distance between you and your opponent, try incorporating indirect attack, attacks that employ fakes which will set up your techniques.

I've found that an attack is easier to detect from a stationary stance than from a moving position; therefore I always incorporate movement to disguise my attacks.

HOW DO I FIGHT SOMEONE WHO HAS A QUICK BACKFIST?

The best strategy against a backfist is to utilize your back hand to block the backfist. Simply open the glove on your backhand and place it 6 to 12 inches in front of your face in a direct line with your opponent's backfist. Keep your front arm against your body, protecting it from reverse punches.

About The Author

Keith Vitali played a key role in the awakening of public interest to semi-contact karate. His presence and performances recharged semi-contact tournaments with the vitality they lacked. For three consecutive years, 1978-1980, he was the number one U.S. semi-contact fighter, and has joined the elite list of America's great tournament fighters; Mike Stone, Chuck Norris, Joe Lewis and Bill Wallace.

Since his retirement from the tournament scene, Vitali has worked as an expert commentator for the Entertainment Sports Network and USA Cable Network, appeared on national TV commercials, worked as a stuntman in *Force: Five*, co-starred in *Revenge of the Ninja*, and promoted the Vitali All Star Champions. He is a partner with Joe Corley in The Joe Corley Karate Studios, and operates the Keith Vitali Karate Studios in Atlanta, Georgia.